SCIENCE IS EVERYWHERE

SUPER SENSES

Sight, taste, smell, touch and hearing

Rob Colson

Published in paperback in Great Britain
in 2019 by Wayland
Copyright © Hodder and Stoughton, 2018

Wayland
An imprint of Hachette
Children's Group
Part of Hodder and Stoughton
Carmelite House
50 Victoria Embankment
London EC4Y 0DZ

Executive editor: Adrian Cole
Produced by Tall Tree Ltd
Written by: Rob Colson
Designer: Ben Ruocco

ISBN: 978 1 5263 0506 0
10 9 8 7 6 5 4 3 2 1

An Hachette UK Company
www.hachette.co.uk
www.hachettechildrens.co.uk

Printed and bound in China

t-top, b-bottom, l-left, r-right, c-centre,
front cover-fc, back cover-bc
All images courtesy of Dreamstime.com,
unless indicated:
Inside front Grashalex; fc, bc Pablo631;
fctr Radub85; fcbr Peterhermesfurian;
fcbc Egal; fcbl Dvu; bctr, 19tr W.kaveney;
bctl Xalanx; bccr Karelnoppe; 1cl, 25tl
Wavebreakmediamicro; 4-5 Stockshoppe;
6cl Photka; 6br Gunita Reine; 7br
Tomwang112; 8-9c Pixeldigital; 8b,
30b Mexrix; 8bc Designua; 8br, 28tr
Science History Images/Alamy Stock
Photo; 9tl Siraanamwong; 9br Jack309;
10cl Tomatito26; 10-11 Tomatito26; 11tr
Johnandersonphoto; 12t, 29r Aona2303;
12t, 23cr snapgalleria; 13t Seishin90;
14-15 Johnfoto; 15br Yulia Ryabokon;
16-17t Dannyphoto80; 17c Dobs65; 17br
Jomiamke4444; 18c Pablo Fernandez
Rivera; 19bl Oguzaral; 20 Taratata;
20tr Carlanichiata; 20bl Draftmode;
20bc 2day929; 20br Alexpacha; Yulia
Ryabokon; 21tl Designua; 21bl Maocheng,
21br Dannyphoto80; 22l, 31tr Lucian
Coman; 23b Felixcasio; 24cr Edward H.
Adelson; 25br Pzaxe; 25bl Jorgenmac;
26c Andreadonetti; 26b Tribalium;
27tl Gbuglok; 27cr Khunaspix; 27bl
Buckskinman; 28bl Hartphotography;
29tr drmakkoy/iStockphoto.com; 29bl
Chrislorenz; 30tl Moomave; 30cr
Martinedegraaf; 32t Stylephotographs

Every attempt has been made to
clear copyright. Should there be any
inadvertent omission please apply to the
publisher for rectification.

Contents

Sensing the world

Special organs in our bodies send information about the world around us to our brains. Our brains use this information to form a picture of what is going on.

Central nervous system

Consisting of the brain and the spinal cord, this is where information from nerve cells is processed.

Nervous system

The brain receives information from all parts of the body using a **network of nerve cells** called the nervous system. Messages move around your body as

electrical signals

at a speed of up to 430 km/h.

Reaction time

The time it takes for the brain to receive a message from the nervous system and send out a movement in response is called the reaction time. One of the fastest reaction times is our blink reflex, which can react to something in our eyes in about 0.1 seconds.

Peripheral nervous system

This system of nerves connects the rest of the body to the central nervous system.

The longest nerve in the body is the sciatic nerve, which extends from the spinal cord to the big toe.

TRY THIS

To see how quickly your nerves transmit signals, **you will need:**

a whistle, a stopwatch, a tape measure and a group of friends.

Stand in a line and join hands. The first person in the line holds the stopwatch, while the last person holds the whistle. The first person squeezes the hand of the person next to them and starts the stopwatch at the same time. As soon as they feel their hand squeezed, each person squeezes the hand of the person next to them, and so on along the line. When the last person feels the squeeze, they blow the whistle and the watch is stopped.

What happened? The nerve signal has travelled up the arm to the brain, which sends the signal to squeeze down the other arm. By measuring the distance from one arm to the other you can measure the total distance the signal has travelled.

5

Seeing the light

Our sense of vision detects a form of energy called electromagnetic radiation, which we usually call light. For humans, vision is the most important sense and a large part of the brain is dedicated to processing information from our eyes.

The eye

Our eyes take in light through the pupil and create an

upside down

image on the retina. The information is sent to the brain by the optic nerve. The brain turns it into an image that is the right way up.

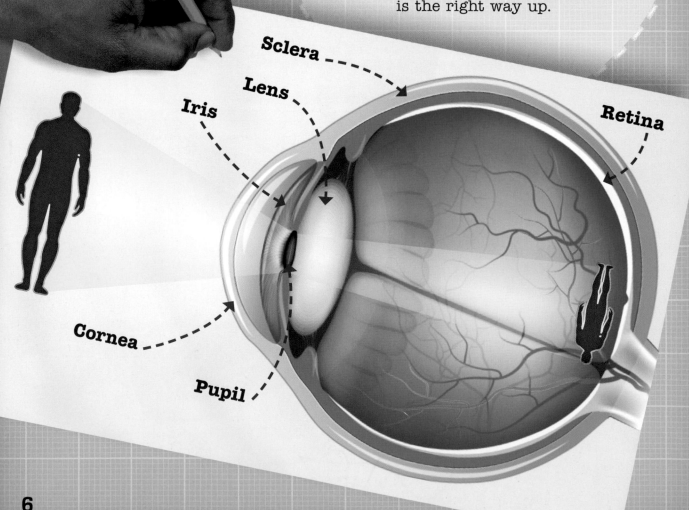

Sclera

Lens

Iris

Retina

Cornea

Pupil

TRY THIS

Hold a finger in front of your face and look at it with each eye closed in turn. The finger appears to change position relative to the background because each eye is seeing it from a **different angle**. Now look at the finger with both eyes, and focus on it. You will see one finger, but two out-of-focus images of the background. Focus on the background, and you'll see two images of the finger. This is known as **binocular vision**, and it helps us to sense how far away something is.

Correcting vision

Some people need to wear glasses to focus the image on their retinas. **Short-sighted** people cannot focus on images that are **far away**. This is normally because their eyes have

grown slightly

too long,

meaning that the lens focuses light in front of the retina. **Long-sighted** people cannot focus on images that are **close-by**. Many people become long-sighted when they get older because the lenses in their eyes have grown stiff.

"That was easy reading!"

A world of colour

Electromagnetic radiation comes in waves of different wavelengths. The range of wavelengths is called the electromagnetic spectrum. Our eyes can only sense a small part of the electromagnetic spectrum. This is visible light, and ranges in colour from violet to red – across all the colours of a rainbow.

Light from the Sun

The Sun gives off **electromagnetic radiation** in all wavelengths, but the most intense ones are in the visible light range.

INFRARED LIGHT

Rods and cones

The retina contains two kinds of light sensor. **The rods provide our night-vision**, sensing light at low levels, but only in black and white. **Cones need brighter light**, but can **sense more detail** and also **sense colour**. Most of the rods are found on the outside of the retina. At night, when you're looking at a dim star, try looking at it out of the corner of your eye. You should see it more clearly.

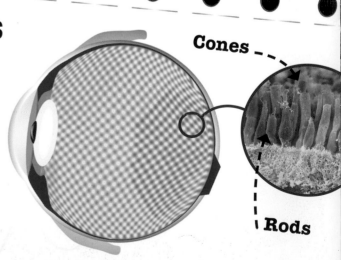

Cones

Rods

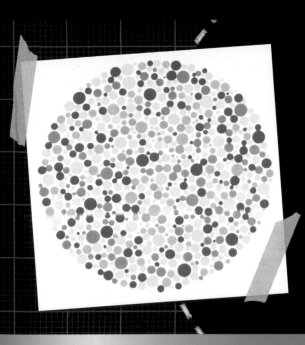

Colour-blind

In most human eyes, there are three kinds of cone cell, each most sensitive to one of **green, red or blue.** Some people lack one or more of these cones, so cannot sense certain colours. The most common form of colour blindness is an inability to tell the difference between red and green. If you are red-green colour blind, you will not see the number 7 in the image on the left.

VISIBLE LIGHT

ULTRAVIOLET LIGHT

TRY THIS

The region around the optic nerve creates a hole in the image on the retina. Normally we are not aware of this hole as our brains fill in the space. To find your blind spot, draw a small cross on the right-hand side of a piece of paper, then draw a dot about 20 cm to the left. Close your right eye and hold the paper at arm's length. Look at the cross with your left eye and slowly bring the paper towards you, being sure to keep looking at the cross. **At what point does the dot disappear?**

Blind spot

Weird eyes

Many animals have very different kinds of eyes compared to humans. They see the world in a very different way from us.

Compound eyes

Insects, such as dragonflies, have compound eyes. Each eye is made of up to **30,000 tiny lenses** that focus light on one point. The insect sees an image that is more coarse-grained than our vision, but it is very good at detecting movement as an image passes from one point on its vision to another.

"I'm glad I don't wear glasses."

Spider eyes

Spiders have between **four** and **eight** eyes. The jumping spider has a row of four eyes at the front of its head, with four more at the back. The smaller outer eyes detect the **movement** of prey such as flies, at which point the spider turns its head and the two larger central eyes zero in on the prey.

Mantis shrimp

Probably the most powerful eyes in the animal kingdom belong to the mantis shrimp. Compared to our three different kinds of cone, mantis shrimps have an incredible 16. They can **rotate each eye** independently to look all around themselves at once.

Colours

Dogs have only two kinds of colour sensor, meaning that they see the world in a similar way to a human with red-green colour blindness. Many birds have a fourth kind of sensor that can sense **ultra-violet light.** Their bright feathers look even more colourful to each other than they do to us.

Only the two central eyes can move. The outer eyes are fixed in place.

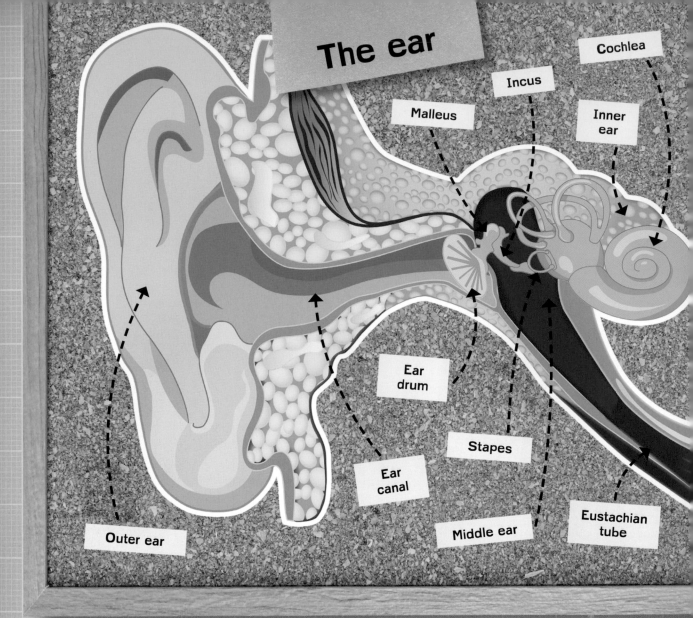

The ear

Malleus

Incus

Cochlea

Inner ear

Ear drum

Stapes

Ear canal

Middle ear

Eustachian tube

Outer ear

Listening out

Our ears detect vibrations in the air in the form of sound waves. Sounds are collected by our outer ears and make our eardrums vibrate. The middle ear transfers sounds from the eardrum to the inner ear across three tiny bones called the ossicles (malleus, incus and stapes). In the inner ear, tiny hairs in a shell-like organ called the cochlea detect sounds and send signals to the brain.

Light and sound

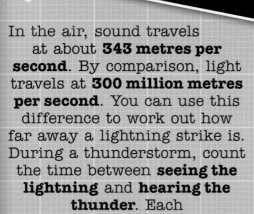

In the air, sound travels at about **343 metres per second**. By comparison, light travels at **300 million metres per second**. You can use this difference to work out how far away a lightning strike is. During a thunderstorm, count the time between **seeing the lightning** and **hearing the thunder**. Each

three seconds

equals one kilometre of distance.

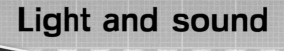

TRY THIS

We use both ears to work out where a sound is coming from. Our brains measure the difference in the time it takes the sound to reach each ear in order to work out exactly what direction and how far away it must have come from.

Mark an X on the floor and measure out distances from the X at **2**, **4**, **6** and **8 metres**. Blindfold a friend and stand them on the X. Now stand at each of the marked distances and say their name. They must tell you which distance you are at. Repeat for all the distances, but with one of your friend's ears covered. **Were they more accurate when using both ears?**

Underwater sounds

Sound waves can travel through any substance. Sound travels

four times

more quickly through **water** than **through air**. Sound can travel huge distances through the oceans and remain audible. Some whales can hear each other's calls from **thousands of kilometres** away.

The sound of music

The musical scale

If we hear two sounds and one has a wavelength that is double the other, we hear these as the **same note,** but the note with the shorter wavelength sounds higher. They are said to be **one octave apart**. On a piano keyboard, each eighth **white key** is **one octave higher**.

Like light waves, sound waves have different wavelengths.
We hear these wavelengths as pitch, or notes.

Musical qualities

When a musical instrument plays a note, the main frequency (called the **fundamental**) is combined with frequencies at higher pitches called

harmonics.

The harmonics have frequencies that are exact multiples of the fundamental. Different combinations of harmonics produce a quality known as timbre. The larger the range of harmonics, the less 'pure' a note sounds.

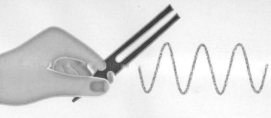

Tuning fork: A tuning fork makes a very pure-sounding note with no harmonics.

Clarinet: A clarinet makes a richer, more harsh sound than a tuning fork, with pronounced harmonics.

Hammer: The sound of a hammer banging contains lots of different frequencies mixed up together. We hear this not as one note, but as noise.

Touch

Our sense of touch is produced by millions of nerve endings in the bottom layer of our skin. These nerves send signals to the brain, telling it whether a surface is rough or smooth, and hot or cold.

In the brain

Our brains process the touch sense in the **somatosensory cortex**, arranged in order from toes at the top to the mouth at the bottom. Next to this is the **motor cortex**, which sends out messages to muscles in these areas.

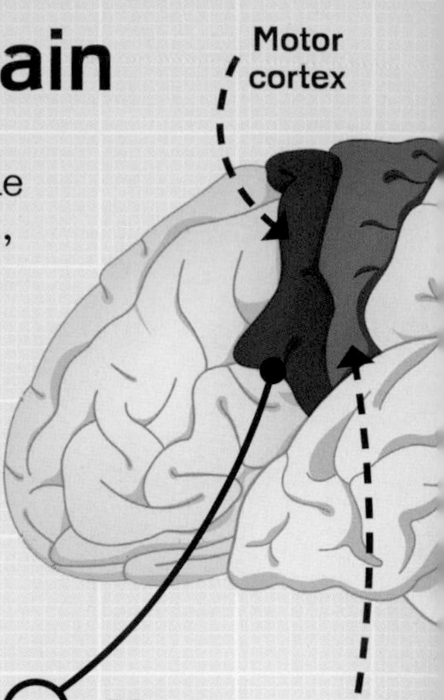

Motor cortex

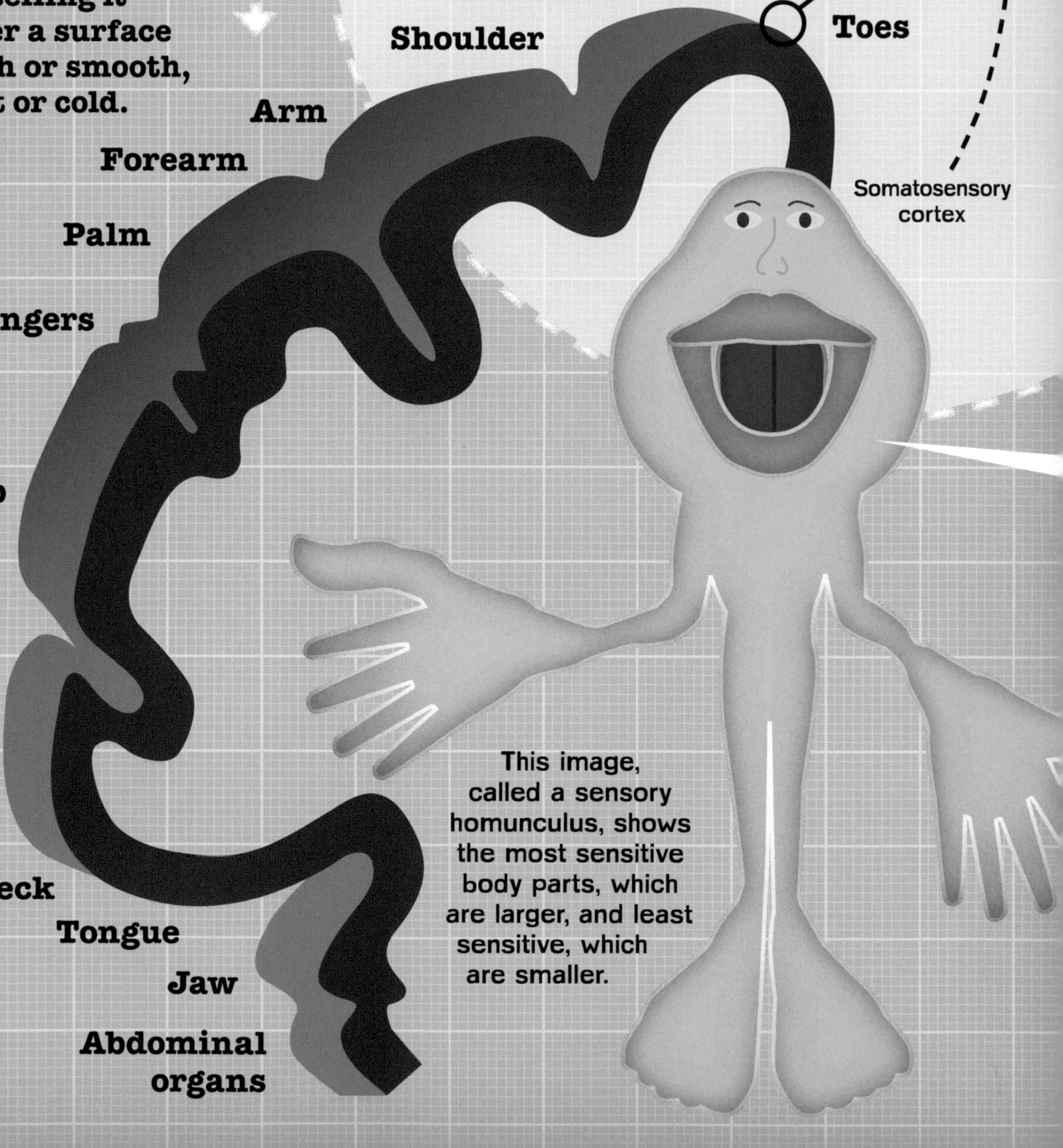

Somatosensory cortex

Abdomen

Leg

Shoulder

Toes

Arm

Forearm

Palm

Fingers

Thumb

Eyelid

Face

Lips

Neck

Tongue

Jaw

Abdominal organs

This image, called a sensory homunculus, shows the most sensitive body parts, which are larger, and least sensitive, which are smaller.

Adapting to the cold

Receptors called **thermoreceptors** sense changes in temperature. After a while, we become used to different temperatures and these receptors stop

sending signals.

When we swim in a cool sea or pool, the water eventually stops feeling so cold. We may occasionally feel currents of warmer water around us. These currents are often less than 1°C warmer than the surrounding water.

"Hey I'm big boned."

Feeling pain

Pain is our body's

warning system.

We avoid painful things, and this keeps us safe. Special pain receptors across our bodies **send messages to the brain** when they detect something that is causing damage to our bodies.

TRY THIS

To see how sensitive to roughness our fingers are, you'll need a selection of sheets of sandpaper of different grades (roughness). You can buy these from a hardware shop. Cut the paper into pieces about 10 centimetres square and write down the grade on the back of each piece. Shuffle the pieces and place them rough-side up. Now close your eyes and use your finger to test each one. Line them up in order from smoothest to roughest. **Did you make any mistakes? At what grade of sandpaper did you go wrong?**

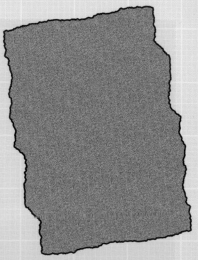

A world of smells

Our sense of smell detects tiny particles of different substances in the air. These particles dissolve in a sticky mucus in our noses. Here, receptors called hair cells detect them and send signals to our brains.

Olfactory bulb at the front of the brain detects smells

Hair cells lead to nerve bundles

Nasal cavity

Different hair cells are sensitive to different chemicals. Human noses have about

40 million hair cells.

There are about 400 different kinds of cell, which means that we can detect many different combinations of chemicals. Scientists calculate that we can distinguish at least **1 trillion different odours**!

Super smellers

Dogs have an incredible **sense of smell**. Their noses have up to **10 billion hair cells**, and a large part of their brains is dedicated to working out what the smells are. A dog's wet nose helps its sense of smell by

dissolving smell molecules.

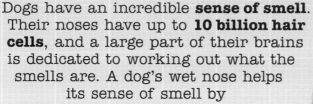

Smell the fear!

Smells have a big effect on our feelings. **Pleasant smells** such as baked muffins or freshly mown grass can instantly make us feel good. We may also be able to smell when others are feeling afraid, picking up on chemicals in their sweat.

TRY THIS

"Is it safe yet?"

Each of us has our own individual smell. A bit like a fingerprint, our **'smell print'** is unique. To test out whether we can identify our own smell, take three clean t-shirts and give one each to three different people. Ask them to wear the t-shirt for a few hours and give them back to you. Now mix the t-shirts up and ask them to close their eyes and identify which one they wore by smelling them.

19

Taste

Our sense of taste allows us to work out which things are good to eat.

We can only sense five basic tastes:

sweet

bitter

sour

salty

Taste hairs detect dissolved substances

Sensory cells react to tastes

On the surface of our tongues and other parts of the mouth are about

10,000
taste buds,

each containing receptors for the five different tastes. Each sensory cell within a taste bud is most sensitive to just one of the basic tastes. The brain combines the information from all the taste buds to create a

sense of flavour

that is a particular combination of the five basic tastes. Thousands of different combinations are possible.

Taste bud

Nerves carry information to the brain

TRY THIS

Our sense of taste depends not only on our tongues but also on our noses. To see the role smell plays in tasting, take three different fruit flavours of jelly bean. Ask a friend to close their eyes and give them a bean of each flavour in turn. Ask them to chew the beans and guess the flavour. Now do the same thing, but have them pinch their nose as they chew. For a third test, crush jelly beans of the same flavour in three plastic bags and ask your friend to breathe deeply from each bag and guess the flavour. How did pinching the nose affect the results? How well did they do when just using their sense of smell? With just taste, we can only sense the sweetness of the beans. We need to be able to smell them to produce a full sense of their flavour.

umami
or savoury

Sensing ourselves

As well as sensing the outside world, we also sense our own bodies. This is known as proprioception. It is produced by sensors in our muscles and joints, which tell the brain how long the muscles are and what angle the joints are at. Combining this information, the brain can work out where everything is.

Barefoot brain booster

When we run and walk, our feet are the **only parts of our body** that touch the ground, and we use information from

nerves on the soles of our feet

to **keep our balance**. Wearing shoes reduces the information coming from our feet. To test this, close your eyes and stand on one leg barefoot then again wearing a trainer with a cushioned sole. **Which is easier?** Running barefoot may even help to sharpen our thinking. When we run barefoot, we must pay attention to where we place our feet, and we are much more aware of our surroundings.

Training for many martial arts is usually done barefoot. Performing high kicks requires balance and coordination.

TRY THIS

Close your eyes and hold both hands above your head. Keep your left hand and fingers completely still. With the index finger of your right hand, swiftly touch your nose and then touch the thumb of your left hand. Touch your nose again, then touch the index finger of your left hand. Repeat swiftly for each finger on the left hand. **Try it a few times. Do you get better?** Now repeat the whole thing, but this time wiggle the fingers on your left hand. Wiggling your fingers gives your brain extra information about exactly where they are, so it should make this task a lot easier.

Dizzy spells

Inside our inner ears are three liquid-filled **semi-circular canals**, which help us to sense movement. When the liquid moves, we feel that we are moving. When we spin around, the liquid eventually starts to spin with us, and we no longer feel that we are spinning, but rather that the world is spinning around us. If we stop spinning suddenly, the **liquid continues to move** for some time. That makes us dizzy, which is the feeling that you are moving when you are not.

"I think I'm gonna be sick."

Fooling the senses

Our brains construct images of the world using information from the senses, but the information is incomplete and the brain fills in the gaps using certain rules. Illusions use these rules to fool our brains into thinking that something is there when it is not.

Optical illusions

Optical illusions fool our sense of vision. In this illusion, **square A** is the

same shade

as **square B**. If you don't believe this, cover up the squares around them to check. Because we think square B is **in shade**, our brains think that it must really be **lighter** than it appears.

Can you see a triangle?
It isn't really there, but our brains interpret the image as a large triangle that sits on top of other shapes.

Auditory illusions

Auditory illusions fool our sense of hearing. When we hear spoken words, **our brains fill in any small gaps** in the information from our ears, so that we may hear a word that hasn't actually been spoken. Researchers at the University of Wisconsin produced a recording in which the speaker coughs mid-sentence and doesn't say part of one of the words. When we listen to the recording, we hear both the cough and the whole word.

TRY THIS

One of the oldest ways to fool your sense of touch is known as the Aristotle illusion. Cross the index and middle finger of one hand then touch the end of your nose. Does it feel like you are touching two noses? Your nose touches the outside of each finger, and your brain fails to take into account that you have crossed them. It interprets this as two separate objects.

More fool you!

The heavy box illusion fools our expectations. Take two boxes, **one large** and **one small** and put an identical brick inside each box. Check that they weigh the same then ask someone to lift them. Most people will say that the smaller box is heavier. We expect the larger box to be heavier, and when we discover that it isn't, we **over-compensate** and think the smaller box is heavier than it is.

Strange senses

Some animals have extra senses that we do not have to help them to find their way around.

Sensing echoes

Bats and dolphins have a sense called **echolocation**, which is similar to sonar. They send out rapid sets of high-pitched clicks and listen out for their echoes when they bounce off objects. The time the sound takes to arrive back at their ears allows them to work out how far away the object is.

Emitted wave of bat

Reflected wave of prey

Bat echolocation is so accurate that it allows bats to catch tiny insects that they cannot see with their eyes.

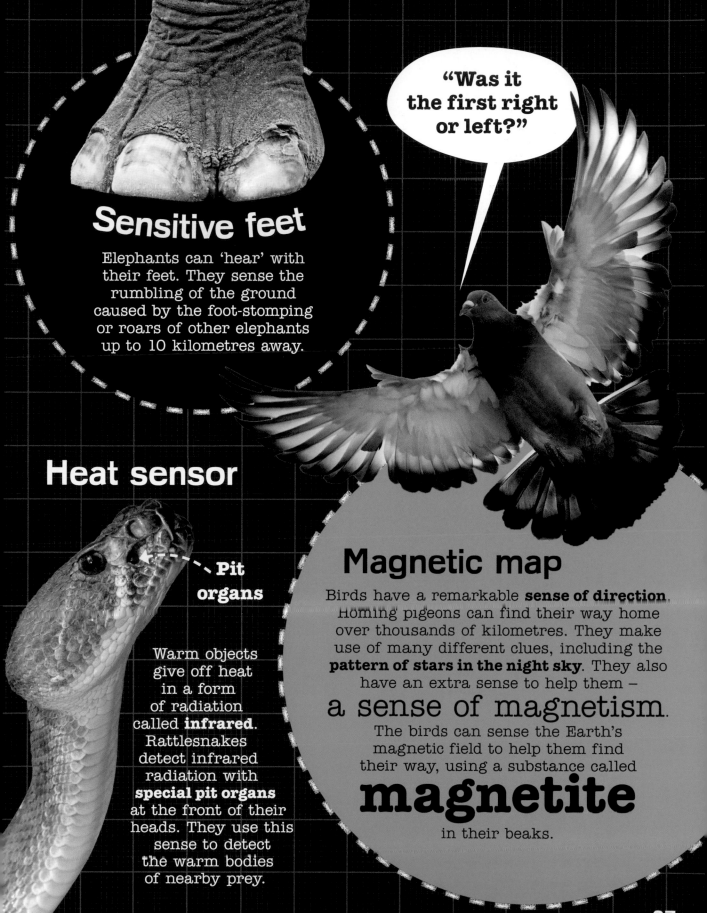

Sensitive feet

Elephants can 'hear' with their feet. They sense the rumbling of the ground caused by the foot-stomping or roars of other elephants up to 10 kilometres away.

"Was it the first right or left?"

Heat sensor

Pit organs

Warm objects give off heat in a form of radiation called **infrared**. Rattlesnakes detect infrared radiation with **special pit organs** at the front of their heads. They use this sense to detect the warm bodies of nearby prey.

Magnetic map

Birds have a remarkable **sense of direction**. Homing pigeons can find their way home over thousands of kilometres. They make use of many different clues, including the **pattern of stars in the night sky**. They also have an extra sense to help them –

a sense of magnetism.

The birds can sense the Earth's magnetic field to help them find their way, using a substance called

magnetite

in their beaks.

Quiz

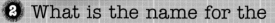

1 As they become much older, most people become

long-sighted.

What causes this?
a) Their eyeballs shrink
b) The optical nerve is damaged
c) The lenses in their eyes become stiff

"Yeah, give me a minute."

2 What is the name for the

sensors

in the eye that detect **detail** and **colour?**
a) Rods
b) Cones
c) Bulbs

3 **Nerves send messages** around the body in the form of what kind of

signal?

a) Electrical signals
b) Radio signals
c) Sound waves

4 Which part of the **electromagnetic**

spectrum

can be seen by many birds but not by humans?
a) Infrared
b) Ultraviolet
c) Microwave

5 Which of the following statements best describes the sound made by this

sound wave?

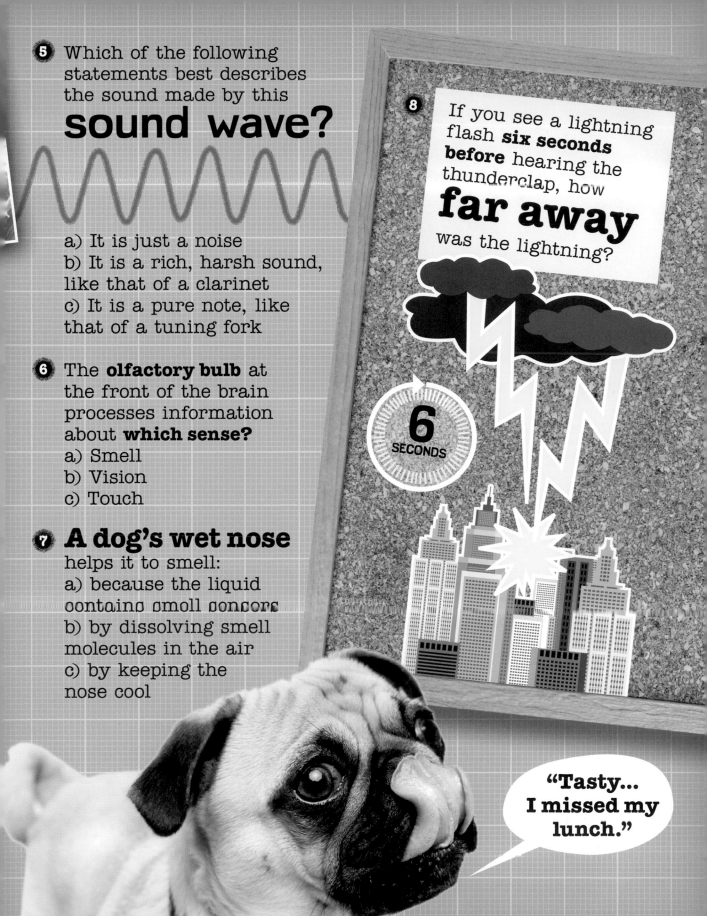

a) It is just a noise
b) It is a rich, harsh sound, like that of a clarinet
c) It is a pure note, like that of a tuning fork

6 The **olfactory bulb** at the front of the brain processes information about **which sense?**
a) Smell
b) Vision
c) Touch

7 **A dog's wet nose** helps it to smell:
a) because the liquid contains smell sensors
b) by dissolving smell molecules in the air
c) by keeping the nose cool

8 If you see a lightning flash **six seconds before** hearing the thunderclap, how **far away** was the lightning?

6 SECONDS

"Tasty... I missed my lunch."

9 We feel dizzy after we **spin round** because liquid is moving in which sense organ?

a) Nose   b) Ears   c) Eyes

10 Thermoreceptors in the skin **detect changes** in what?

a) Temperature
b) Humidity
c) Light

11 Name the **five basic tastes** that our **tongues** can detect.

12 In addition to the tongue, which other **sense organ** is important to our sense of taste?

13 **Look at the following image**. Which of these three statements is **true?**

a) Vertical line A is longer than vertical line B
b) Vertical line B is longer than vertical line A
c) The two vertical lines are the same length

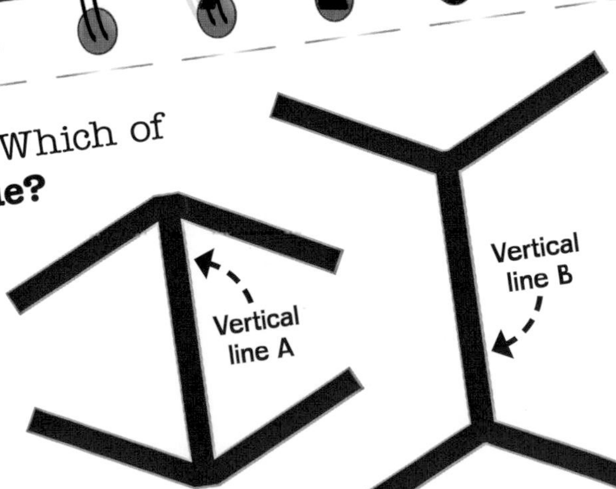

Vertical line A

Vertical line B

Glossary

Blind spot
The point at which the optic nerve joins the retina. It is insensitive to light so causes a gap in our vision.

Central nervous system
Consisting of the brain and the spinal cord, this is the place where information from the rest of the body is processed.

Cochlea
A shell-like organ in the inner ear, which detects sounds and sends signals to the brain.

Compound eye
An eye made up of thousands of tiny lenses. The more lenses the eye has, the more detail it can see.

Electromagnetic radiation
A form of energy that travels in waves of different wavelengths.

Frequency
The number of times a wave, such as a light wave or sound wave, oscillates or vibrates in a second.

Illusion
An effect that fools our senses into believing that something is there when it is not there.

Infrared
A form of electromagnetic radiation that has a longer wavelength than visible light. Heat is often given off in the form of infrared radiation.

Long-sighted
Unable to focus on objects that are nearby.

Nerve cell
A cell that carries electrical signals. The brain is made up of billions of nerve cells, and a system of nerves extends right around the body.

Organ
A part of the body that carries out a specific task or set of tasks.

Peripheral nervous system
The network of nerve cells that carries messages between the central nervous system and the rest of the body.

Proprioception
The sense of where our own bodies are in space and how they are moving.

Receptor
An organ or cell in the body that senses a change in qualities, such as light or heat, and sends a signal to the brain.

Retina
The area at the back of the eye on which an image is formed. The image is upside-down.

Short-sighted
Unable to focus on distant objects.

Spinal cord
A bundle of nerve cells that runs from the brain down through the back.

Index

Answers

1. c) The lenses in their eyes become stiff.
2. b) Cones
3. a) Electrical signals
4. b) Ultraviolet
5. c) It is a pure note, like that of a tuning fork.
6. a) Smell
7. b) by dissolving smell molecules in the air.
8. It was two kilometres away.
9. b) Ears
10. a) Temperature
11. Sweet, sour, bitter, salty and umami (savoury)
12. The nose
13. c) This is an optical illusion. The two vertical lines are the same length.